# waiting to connect...

poetry by Scott Cooper

ISBN 1-58776-047-9
Library of Congress Card Number 00-103047
An original Publication of Vivisphere Publishing.
Printed in the U.S.A.

**Straw House Press**
Vivisphere Publishing
a Division of NetPub Corporation
2 Neptune Road, Poughkeepsie, NY  12601

www.vivisphere.com

for:

℗	Mom and Dad...who shaped me into happiness
	with pride and freedom...

℗	the southside agents, the cricket, Mary & Ryan,
	Kristen & Louis...true friends

℗	Iris, Creations and the New Paltz heretics...who
	showed me the range of expression...

℗	Teal...for life and love

# Contents

"The complex of succesively experienced informations produces interweaving episodes--and the complex of special-case-episode-interweavings produces the scenario that our brain's memory banks identify as our individual being's 'life.'"

R. Buckminster Fuller

waiting to connect...

*a life*

all I am
is debris
falling around a dream
moistened by the tears of the sky
and washed away


. . . . .

remember me ... i'm the time

that forgotten slice of movement
called a boundary

a swift tunnel of perspective
that ebbs coolly in the back of minds

both finite and vague
bubbling the cauldron of your science

spicing the courses of imagination
without end

those who ride me
find love in a breath

those who shun
fall victim to eternity


I am deeper than a word
I am smaller than a person
I am smarter than the sand
I am the marriage of all relation


. . . . . .

smoothed out the crush
conglomeration
pattern meeting
firecrackers and UFO's
blessing water
holy wine
drunk in features
and candy lick
meet me in a simple garden
stalking petals
mood colors
eaten before time knew tick

all the beauty
each fallen lock
curly with surprise
smiles at the coming wind

caught again
another she
a boisterous voicestress
braided angel
cool and comfortable

without the control and freedom
of the sun
we are held in our waking mood
for the duration
(pushing against these sticky, padded walls)

. . . . . .

they cannot heal me

marauders
slick enough to steal nothing
and be a criminal


. . . . .

a longer season than the sun could help
too many steamy operations frozen in a slow melt
no sense of standard time
winters are always of
mind
emotions
relations
fire-place sensations
building invisible walls

then spring reaches out
grows the height
asks if we wish to climb
away to the new brilliance

now is the real consternation
to let go of these nectar blood wounds and wonders
or stay within the molted skin          protected
     even to be blind of the          whole

but through the awareness and aptitude of friends
the desire to really breathe air already swirling around
shedding begins      to free your range of motion

(but) time is no angel here
no true reporter
those sands become something different
once fallen
   all the suggestions
feeble castles
shape     your potential

the sinister ancient
hold their breath
collect ...
rip out the wind(s)
sending the dreams
edge by edge
back into following

. . . . .

a spiritual peasant
sowing early seeds
on to and fro
wishes
walls of impasse
fortify a small world
both cold and comfortable
to see the distinct ways
can only shatter
paper
thin dimensions
while the murky moats
of indiscretion and foul blinders
sink deep the thoughts
of freedom

so to arise from
this ignorant lake
without fresh sight
leads a wary eye

this cannot shimmer
the many paths do not
illuminate for ease
rather hide in the shadows
of those you light....


. . . . .

all I know
everything I remember
time is a fragment
I can't replace

and the things
I do to remain sane
fall out of the sky
        so much rain

and the things
that people say to get their way
burning their mouths
with truth decay

all I see
everything I uncover
life is a moment
with too much space

and my love
that calls me out and runs away
doesn't know god
but prays anyway


and the last thing I recall
the bouncing of the ball
the leaves
their flight
and fall
and then the winter
just like my everyday
long gone

. . . . .

apparently it's the time
apparently things level themselves into creaseless blank paper

movies are teaching me about myself
and all around me

now I'm scared

the metaphysics and self-help don't
turn my pages
squeezing the wisdom from our off base contemporaries

I'm scared at what makes me cry
though I love to cry

I'm scared of what makes me scared
though it may never happen again

I'm afraid that everything really does make sense.


. . . . .

as you enter the throne of the Basilica

a cold history raps into the long connected existence
no longer woman or man
but descendant of now stone frozen idols
and scarcely clothed representations

lit now by candle and starry eyed visitors
it appears possible that our smallness is underestimated

all the streets of my Chicago bear the emotion
of a single tile on this floor

these are chiseled gateways for
every idea
mystery
and fallen hero

we revisit anguish here
along with the old fear of such a higher power

our circuits are not powered this way
no one sacrifices
no one kneels

only the temperature of new days can lead us
to the horizons that fated these past breathers
(of silent, servant prayers)


. . . . .

but she's not calling my name
it's just the wishing
and the Jazz...
sifting through the rotten pile of memory

the piano says I'll lose
sight of what's important
(and) the trumpet tells me
it's worth the risk...

. . . . .

caught in my stomach
knotting and plotting
a softly branched sprig of pain

slow pull of lover's rejection
from every direction

confusion is the norm, here
  far too easy
a steady hand
must move to replenish
these hairline fractures
formed to a web of permanent constriction


. . . . .

*troubadour*

chipped edges     aside
worn sunset strings
this instrument ... guitar
on the ground, alone
it's inability
you would find
But     upon
perpendicular limbs
cradled, guided
by hard triumph     soft heart
and fingers forced often to let go
a journey has begun...

dull plucked vibrations
blend and mend
a sweet, honey cracked voice
metered
by the shoe striking
frozen liquid stone
harmony moves from ears to eyes
to this man
an island     from island
melancholy chords
smiling and flying
holding me in an open onyx gaze...
whispers his name beneath the din

and there
swaying in the breeze
of calm revolution
sits my soul
caught in the grip of belief

. . . . . .

*ourglass*

the era cannot contain us
ripples goad time along
in unconnected circles
linear theologies
stagnate the air
we breathe
coincidence
set in the stone
of the stars
eludes the imagination
perhaps the savior
skipped rocks over the water
having the quilted tale
passed over time
until those stones became feet
and the feat became his own

. . . . . .

i'm waning
filed away
an electronic breeze
soul aimed as laser

enterfacing in blind jousts        riding a vapor trail

multicolored identity in flight


. . . . .

*still life*

snap

we are  3 by 5  Kodak  zoom
celebrating the stillness
afraid to move
cause directions point to style
the clock is ticking...

dying from the stress
of
just how late is fashionable

hug and hand over souls
to strangers
with coats and throats
hung in a tiny   quiet   dark room

while the walking, talking skin
play carpet maneuvers
of cocktails and conquest

the night and it's breath
call the curtain (to freedom)
and the path to your back
becomes the blade's flight

good night

. . . . .

*departure*

she was (of)
soft winged flights of the heart
within our history, brief

joined to travel
carriages of thought and passion
(then) to bask in the light of near death
in our throw away lives

now the vessel of my love is telepathic
as a great sea divides

and waves our good-byes

. . . . .

*the gap*

always pushing to the back
gather in minority
to engage a unique
pleasure in revolt

family enters
masked in normality
2.5 in tow
barking hot chocolate wishes
to copy adult coffee

father wanders from the flock
eyeing style and structure
matriarch chats and corrals
quietly questioning quality
and stubbing smokers with her gaze...

yet the boundary is peaceful
this gap of
when you were and when we weren't
isn't
at all

no one is angry...

no
one
is
angry

. . . . .

*three heel clicks*

and the ceiling became a grid
intersecting points of origin
so we
call home a faraway place
rare and disturbing


. . . . .

now
you may be in your bed
this night
wrapped in familiar blankets
and pillows
smelling of fresh mom
now
free of my searching, cold feet
and the suckling black kitten

out where the towering rock
offer safety, no escape

soon the wings of dark and night
steal you away to me
together in the conscious underground
we hold on
grasp what the light
will not give us

. . . . .

*a motion*

on the wave
so fine the crest
bare of origin
invisible of end

knowing no clock
no frustration

ships of steel and feather
ride your skin

and still there is peace

the sun, your friend
sees itself in you
as we all do

your quiet
forces us to listen
remember
sadden
rejoice
and remain

how have you retained your way?

your secret ... sweet water
sweet love

· · · · ·

## *Pub Joust*

I
visualize the thunder
standing with
Thor's narrow hammer
in hand...
a glance around the room
stirring suspense
aligning ghostly orb...
burning an eyeward path
while the tightly packed
rainbow ivory await
and I'm bent over the felt romper
ready
where's that sound...
the solid descent into the chasm,
calculated roll to banishment...
always anticipating
that chance bump and drop
succumbing of the black specter...
as rare as all instant success

not so,
one down,
stripe backed crimson...
left with chaotic spread
and unchangeable lie
geometric divisions aglow

smell that
air of confidence

as the music's got me
captured
by the jive table strut...

one more surely fired
into the cave
and the second quickly
knocked astray...

opponent's eyes light fire
ablaze in expectancy...
vulture-like circular stalk
about the green surface
one, two, three more
sentenced to temporary  incarceration...

but odds against
the next pull short...
I'm activated once more
concentration automatic
balls whispering instruction...

but on this turn they' be no smoke
or fanfare
the enemy takes his cue
and I,  stand and watch...
within moments
all but the last are left
pressure mounts the emptiness
and my rival falls victim...

riding the wave of necessity
I clear all
to leave but one...
the ominous shadow
stands fast and confident

that interwoven insignia of eternity
staring down...
daring me to divine its destiny
while underneath jukebox rhythms
the distinct vexing murmurs of my adversary
rise to the surface...

having finally chosen an approach
I slither into position...
attentive
and
aroused
by the cool aiming sex of the stick
slid amid the tight crux of fingers...

climax coming with the release...
and measured strike...

so little time for imagination
between the meeting
of these paradoxical spheres...

reaction swift
idle commentary following the finish
hands shake foes to friends
and weapons placed on empty battleground

the new competitor ... lurking
plotting the overthrow of my victorious show
and I ... ready again

"Rack 'em"

. . . . .

# Surrend-Her

through a fortified facade
built of battles before
invisible tears tore at the core
and the more …

pieces of panicked heart in her pockets
empty lockets of a hundred mothers
in her sockets

for she knew her support
though wise
could not protect    her child
from the possible demise

her eyes
had wished so dearly
that maybe one
This One
sweet child of creation fair
could dance lightly among us
without impair

Nay
'tribulation is the teacher'
we would say
inflicting trials on careless smiles
before they trek  … life's hard enough miles

How Dare We!
without repose
steal the prose from under the nose
of those
for without fear
no hate in babe grows

her eyes

stuck between the now and then
sent countless cries of

... not again ...


. . . . .

*make the grade*

the fiber is not gently laid, this day
our romantic visions of beauty and joy
filter through the lens of jagged edges
and glimpses of the future

to make the limit of art
a rectangle
flat    defiant
belies a certainty of what is to come
an arrogance of the substance of now
we have that no more

lines are dimensions
thick with world and life
color is emotion
subtle and present
shape cannot rely
on its own merits
within the science of soul

only the instant is defended
with arms and honesty

this is all a trick
the utmost deception waits behind every presence
paying attention cannot defeat the mirrors
of sly handed mind emperors
seeking the definition of non bordering existence
so
sleep with the blue of sorrow
smile on the green breath
walk through the halls of fluctuation

this is not a test.

. . . . .

*the limit*


the screen is blinking
computer humming
chair is rolling
cigarette burning
coffee brewing
cat is purring
music playing
phone ringing
car is running
wind blowing
sun shining


still the limit is you ...


. . . . . .

ear to the wind
their slights reach me
as wavelengths
minor punctuation
within the energy of each waiting

others are circling
just now learning
chattable fence talk
they are the instigators
of exponential information spread


. . . . .

energy leaches provide nothing but distortion
simple conversations on simple days
they are plotless anticlimactic boozehounds of verbal ale
  static in their listening

short wicked brooders circle them
with condensed years of attention
in the end
snapping loose the jabbering leach logic

further the aimless revolutionaries
wrinkle the fabric of all
constantly reshaping their political playdoh perceptions
for the sake of contrast

a disharmonious chorus
these skin and bone seesaws
stomachs turning on the way up
teeth clapping jolt to the ground

these are my Platos
  these are my Einsteins
these are the mothers and fathers
  of my realing understanding

. . . . . .

in her smile
caught wind
translucent insectile wings
waving urgently
to escape the point

attracted to the moisture
of despair
a buzzing huddle
of herk jerk intersection

we know flight
the meeting
and the swoon
first touches
difficult   till tomorrows

staying...
though
is not carried
on the shoulders of inspiration

. . . . .

even this book has control over me
the music discs demand attention
feign a stolid jealousy
slick and wired
an echelon of the world call to me softly
spicing the already wearing
wounds my psyche endures
smooth buzz knows my name
as well
the omnipresent escape-hatch
a cumulous shroud
easily assumed
dull of blade
but sharper than the House

• • • • •

everyday to try and enact
something more than talking
these the days of advancement
where we can all be water-walkers

everyday I look around
spy the flow of evidence
as each action ripples farther out, around
flooding the pools of creative perception

everyday it becomes more clear
angels are a dime a dozen
time truly caresses us



. . . . .

don't any importance
 to what gain
support kindled blaze
 answers inherit minds
  will
my
 question merit finds


    (space regulates conversation)


don't any importance
 to where vain
distort critical phase
  EARTH   life is alone
 will
my
    Dog (star) find a bone


    (time is litigation)



spiral staircases


. . . . . .

under the protective cover
of lush aged pine
a porch, a perch
sagging rust colored beams of wood
grunting under the weight of soft chairs and primitive steps

the place to be

and then the night
basketballs bounce to still
plastic bats laid to rest
in a cool bed of grass

replaced by
wooden rhythm sticks
and steel corded electric axes
turning
the sunlit social scene
to smoky basement radio
with a heartbeat
and something to prove

from the street
a gangly teen slows his car
to bask in the togethered glow
of this house
sitting atop the stale rows of normal life

from the stairs
a tangled lass blows her smoke
to escape the weathered show
of this house
sinking below the pale throes of daily strife

he is now past
shifts to gear
himself up for another night
of aimless roads
envious starts
angered stops

she is sad fast
lifts a tear from
her shelf of lonesome plight
of shameless odes
devious hearts
passion props

the car is dark and quiet
and fire,
the hated door of his home
waiting to grip his hand
cold, brass clutches
ushering inside
locking away the dream (again)...

older and older
stairs glow colder
heart fades weaker
boys grow bolder
their chemistry sleeker
from beaker to beaker
to break her and seek her
hold her and smolder
leaving a bleak and doubt stained shoulder

. . . . .

*climate*

I can smell her reign
coming to an end
the intermittent gray
lifting and falling home

we were such weather
without forecast


. . . . .

forget the cool chase friend
the melting magma
of natural movement(s)
a slick strip strikes
perceptible paths prying
open obvious overtures
beneath between boundaries
defunct dimensional depots
eradicated emotion emitting
linear love liquid
ambrosial aromas asserting
false fetal fornication
mimicking motherly mantras

never nurture need
she says somberly
weaving weather within
cold chaotic conversation

rely   remember   revolt

disappear

. . . . .

further down              below the nil
when the traps have snapped free

you land, no matter how far down
an escape can be seen, envisioned
during the fall
perilous descending
no perspective is available
no action may be taken


. . . . .

fields
     run
        away
          and    I
can only challenge
          the
            surface

          the
            beauty we know

          calls forward

            times

    past


. . . . .

hello again

things have changed
yes
but the echo remains
for me
I
built the time apart
into mystery...
a religion

calling your name
to the sky

arcing comets
carrying wishes

but now
we are interacting voices
spanning the fallen bridge
with the thinnest yarn from our tale

so I came to the middle to meet you

and stood alone

how could one know
we'd outgrown the places that had fit
so perfectly

before

. . . . .

i can only begin to try and connect with the long past years
battled seconds and defended the slimmest of hopes
these tangled vines of succulent fare
full of rhythm
empty to breathable space

leaves are falling now
like they are supposed to

i am falling now


. . . . .

eat through a spoon
tapping a glass
watching
further movements plagiarize
sipping sun coffee
thick with smoke
tying knots out of words
there is always a she
who serves the plate
smiling for cash and forgetting forks
door swings, curtain calls
we know you or don't
we want you or don't
later
we need you or don't
a glass falls
decides to break
maybe even shatter
I'm still hungry
I'll eat the bread now
remember my childhood
and take the check
last sip of coffee      standing

. . . . .

I had wanted it to be special
the kind of thing
that only energy could recognize ...

. . . . .

I remember you
          the tall challenger

just beginning to think about the transparent dimensions
that fold around and between us

gateways that go nowhere
outside the mind


. . . . .

tactile explosion
senses exist beyond the mind
jarring crispness
softening clarity
a heaviness
to plant us in observation
sounds become source-linked information symphonies
alerting, alarming, elating

(the light projected screensaver
of our neuro-computer
sharps everything to its edges
blends with the sound to engage
our further senses of relation
to solidify a true depiction of life's agility)

in observation
slightly detached from body
touch folds into a last line
of defense and research

this molded stone
is lucid and cautious
where a breeze is suspicious
every limb and lash a stranger

body not made for this elevation
soon enough nerves and nodes
rearrange and react
a slow pull through the system
to regain control

(brought back to our seat and feet world)

. . . . . .

if the door is open   lose me in your steps
to move slowly   is binding
an indication
don't be delicious

everything finds its way to peace
naturally
the earth does not decide things
action is truly abhorrent
it negates the flow

the underneath is what amazes

how our blood directs us
like great plates shifting below the crust
connecting and disconnecting
ideas, logic and soul

how events match moments
how the air smells and looks before storm
how eyes glimmer and gloom with detection
how we are how we are now is nowhere new


. . . . .

 in the simplest colors
eyes full and proud
that image of digital voyage
personified my cold, glassy canvas
as she appeared

leaving me unable to close it away
return to the often sterile functions
of this whirring box

freeing herself infinitely through one frozen moment


. . . . .

it was a shadow
  is a shadow
turned
piece of sky blinked
until pregnant enough
to wander away from the weather


. . . . .

it's a wavering tempest
slight, factual
emotion processing
warm like the sun
dances down
tripping artery webs

shafts of light, energy     action
all the voices
angel playground
true children of no god
united in song


. . . . .

love you with greatness
span the distance
leave behind the reaches of doubt
these are not readily accomplished
with easy smiles
and unwavering pen strokes

confidence is the issue
not passion

are we to be linked without rings and vows
locked in ceremony-free wed

no honeymoon or rice strewn paths

only delicate oaths of youth
testing the mettle of our pride and contentment

words too soon fade from
blood pumping visions and action
new kings and queens enter the circle of motion
to rule our devotion

and sure enough pass on as quickly as they came

who will be that permanence
the unbridled yet stoic love
as present and timely as the dawn and close of day...
whose arms and charms
open only for me


can I be as stone as the mold I seek?

. . . . .

(magnetic poetry)

beneath the breast of essential woman
smooth gorgeous whisper of love

above the elaborate storm of man
frantic bitter vision is lust
hot headed language is worshipped

cry
mother
sing

. . . . .

can you really understand
the jazz man
that's a trip plane
moving around
your ears
are you hearing it
feeling it
is it a visible code
you realize
it's the blues
of another dimension


. . . . .

masked behind the perfect visions of love
we are given the stories
supposed hope to last us through our less than perfect lives

we are twisted and turned through
all the styles enjoyed within such sparse imaginations

we are revisited by themes that left us empty so many times before

we applaud even the most remote success in these dead horses


i almost cried tonight
at a movie
i felt the swell of contrived engagement move through me

suppressed this

too often I wish to not give in

these rented moments are not the pinnacles
these are not my heroes

i have felt more love
        seen more sadness
        laughed harder
in a day
with my lover

we write, direct, produce, act
we finance, distribute, and project

all that is needed to see and hear of life and love


. . . . .

my head is gone
attention is pounding in my right ear
the hum is taking over

binary


. . . . .

no urge to explore
physical spaces
she says "accented"
  I body language rebuff
-she hates that-
within me – assumptions
crinkle and crack
I wait till buttons
aren't being pushed
and return


. . . . .

perhaps you're confessing
on paper bird wings
the easy difference
between what you believe
and what is happening


. . . . .

Portal Cafe

squeaky swings of to and fro
blow, blissful breezes  of
know you grins
heartfelt  how've you beens
don't care who wins
just come on ins


spun from social spiders
drunk of cider, smoke and
childhood proof lighters
sparking lovers and fighters
and
should I sit beside hers


it's clear...
we conversate a poem
bounce buoyant banter on our foam


it's here, friends
heretical hats hang like home


. . . . . .

rub until sore against     today
he stood at her sitting
enunciating behind clavicles
the teepees of tension

as always anxious fingers found       yesterday
   balled up fetal
amid muscles we don't know what to call

that reaction   censoring
   that body response

and having never seen Gilbert's grapes
or a real glimpse of languid America

only the cold despondency
of our four digit access
to always one more door to freedom

it's eating in the dark


.  .  .  .  .

she rarely looked up
making the words
bend to me

arriving slightly exhausted


. . . . .

sure the base features lure
realize and magnetize
but underneath that skimmed surface
lies an invisible, gentle predator

a lurking, smirking scent
that draws the laws of
intent and foreshadowing

this form, this sculpted, vaulted image
refurnishes itself at the meekest glance and innuendo

to be wary of your silent instigator


. . . . .

motivation is not automatic
all the strength I garnish
is not enough to conjure a will to action

tiny anthill moments
 smaller steps of larger goals
become stern obstacles

for the courage
to descend and not fall
have the ready balance required
to climb yet again

not new or fresh ideas

it moves in blinks
powershifting defenses
it moves around need and reason
    without trial

two sides of the story
never told by people,
represent good and evil
in every instant
and remain uneditable

smaller days knew
the truer scale
regardless of digression

we, though, in the now
have translated the simplest and most natural
instincts infinitely
forever losing the clarity of wrong ...
the silent victory of right

. . . . .

the shattered  scattered filaments
our light   our idea

swim terra steps
and wander
around the potential
of touching hands

(light fantasies, at best)

now these
warm mental milk concoctions
soothe to sleep
concrete doubts
about the reality      of one day together

a thinning tether made without instruction

this
     is
          tangible waiting


. . . . .

sun comes
brings unnecessary light
to the technological teepee
where ambient colors hum and glow

memories are a click away here
so fast,
fantasy sleeps long
presses only ripping insights

this canvas
a whisper to glass
breezy function
without foretelling or interaction
just binary emotion

we are soon to be archived in this fashion
vibrant recollections of humanity
stored as cold debris and frozen space


. . . . .

the table
  smaller than the talk
buckled under our summing glances

ash fell          smoke rose
knees danced              eyes darted

a low, passionate crossfire
etching grooves in our malleable shields

she was earth
down to the gravel grabbing boots
and dark, soothing hair
smooth and beautiful
as nature's simplest stone

across from her the lankiest tree
swayed in the wind of her voice
full of romance and doubt
with a set of auburn watchers
that melted and cooled every blink

soon
time grew weary of our banter
flinging us closer
to a certain and longstanding good-bye

we moved discreetly
an old fashioned arm held the door
for her exit
into a cold condition of night

hand in hand
  traversing a path
to the contoured chariot
  of her departure

we quickly ducked the traps
  of faulty hope
realized the wisdom of moments
and dove into the succulent honesty

. . . . .

the words...you choose  to use
lose their way

exiling our realistic
with the statistic
of your ballistic

a discordant web of deceit
one can expect
to repeat, repeat

but perhaps
I may say we thank you

for now

landed here from social sifting
hand in hand ... our spirits lifting

warmed in the ears of my peers

in a rented room of regression
with dented doom of depression
satiated in the sex of our expression

you all for me and us
bend and spend a tattered trust
paint each other's pain benign
ferment our blood and tears
to wine

and so
without alas

I raise my glass
a toast

. . . . .

this one particular pen is a richer tonic
than most shirt pocket inhabitors
refilled not with blood      rather
let it find my qualities to liquefy
and represent a journal excreted

. . . . .

transparent winged fairies
cold in the logic of man
flutter and crack
with escape


. . . . .

under his pen
a moment's shape and luster
is captured in sensual archive
he illuminates
the collision of emotion and experience
from his frantic fingers
tiny follicle ideas
explode into blood and breath

there is no need to stray in his world
every blister is exposed, explored
the reality of each blush performed and painted
(meet him once and your ode is eminent)

a true cartographer of human travels
a difficult piper to follow
a soulful scribe
  engaged in spiritual government
battling the rule of our energies


an original existence


. . . . .

under my match
burn

correspondence and image
call to smoke
and rise    away

did we not blaze in this same fashion
a flickering desert orange

air could not have moved between us
  in that

but days and ways
break even bolted bonds

and now

the sex of our soul
billows to form that new yearning spirit
a gaseous babe of contellating light


. . . . .

waiting for you
amidst the play of children
spirited by the vibrance of autumn
while fat squirrels dance and dart through acorn eden

each snapped twig is of your foot
whip and turn of my neck uncontrolled
a moment's importance
to every catcher of my hopeful glance

the dinner hour must be upon
as families flock and file to find
correctly matching mommies and daddies
honking and hailing from steel boxed bubbles of safety

they too  mock your approach
as time drips a two scoop cone
licked up neatly by my anticipation

soon your hair, duskily glistened
will eat the elms of ego with envy

conscious now
surrounded by the sounds
of fathomless faith and tierless trust

sad as the season sings
of how this too will change

cool breeze of reassurance
as it becomes less important
that you are not here...
more that you are coming at all...

(the lesson of fall)

. . . . .

we close ranks fast    here
doors shut behind
coats fall to a mass grave

movement turns to merriment
slight glances
            touches
translate to a damp fiber
that twists and sways
intoxicated

growing stronger
swept into
conversations linked
by smoke and
our thick dialectal reasoning

some are smoother
react to the night
evolve (temporarily)


. . . . .

where others fail
he's got too much breath
for the horn
that sly digit dance
is everytime-forever
standing
parallel to the ground
he pauses

an opportunity
for the mother-plucker
to center stage
rise out from under
the nectarous cover
the air blown oxygen holiday
an active octave session
slides aside, back below
brass earth angel returning
took a walk around the block
back in front
leading
harmony-less    mind travel
where you find your own way


. . . . .

zero is the first moment
  of natural awakening
from this point
   information accumulates
   laying aware, motionless
     observing all senses
     (remaining mute)
the environment, its energy
as motion and data
   link with what survives
the dreamscape

   that infernal machine
   with its uncompromising bones
    instigate order to the day
blinking rearranging
               constantly
tapping shoulder(s)


. . . . . .

movement
  again

 underneath

it's the bubbles
   rising out
of the sandy caverns

(overthenight swellsweeping
disfactual improperties
refinalize organaceous aromacies)

who detects the murky whisper
  two bottle genies
will fish for food

  simple steps   infant words

pretend running away


. . . . .

shapeshifting
          clock       strikes
between us   glossy
postcards

  eating the flow
  narrow triangle tips
fat envy

smooth silent pierce
  angled refract slice

color mama
pancake rebellion
  surprise

all the way
till words
  elusive into spiral
gene core

break down
back beat

. . . . .

made the mistake
allowed them inside
installing vagrant voice-boxes
within once sound proof walls
           are you there?
testing one, two, threee....

bastards
  quiet when I need comforting chatter
babbling through tender moments

only music saves me
   keeps it different

rearranges the innards
reprograms my computer

gives me a new god


. . . . .

sitting in the new bathroom
surrounded by apple scented shampoos and tired mirrors

where prisoners of passion
wash free fertile fluid of allowance

such a kinky kaleidoscope of wishes
compromised and contrasted
by fumbling tongues and cold toes
spearing moans and
regrettable sexual sentence structure

waking to hope
kneeling to the religion of chance
reeling as the next smile is the dance

as partners spin delight
  to blindness

spelling backwards discontent
this new eraser for the past

until zero swoops down
collecting your moment of fear

. . . . .

if the green walls
of this narrow coffee shop
could flex / flux

to represent us in space and thought

if, at times,
the structure of ideas
were too micro
the walls closing in
the ceiling falling
our physical destroyed

if then
the structure of belief
were to expand
convey a volume
we could perhaps reflect
and identify our perfect smallness


. . . . . .

I could easily rip off

                                a head
        light a cigarette
find peace
    that would quickly fragment
        into the kind of thoughts
that make sleep                 fiction


. . . . .

pay attention
        your science is too outward
        remind me                      again
        why the words fly unconnected
those adults
        unavailable
        to organic reasoning
        defy experience teaching
wingless wonders
        peak and valley nomads
        listen to the head winds
        swirling voices of fresh pain

interpreted  … aimed
        "You there!  You can help me!
        Help me          Help
                me
                me

"I don't know you.   You don't know you."

. . . . .

what is left     of
ways you pictured
          all the outcomes

a series of wasted attempts
to prognosticate some future

shuffle the cards
          think of your question

reaching out to glossier fantasies

mystical choose your own adventure

fuck the beads   false leads   and tarot reads

the psychology of astrology
is built on decisions


. . . . .

inside everything I see
whether in dreams or day
the current

weaving its way
on all our transparent cloaks
system of information
clear
defiant
as a concrete truth

together all our wares and weaknesses
intermingling     rising
into a dustbowl of human complexities
a strident role
new aspect for each


. . . . .

there is nothing delicious
left
only a bitter struggle
with ethics and friendship
the sun is
         apparent
moods around continue
their jollities and confusion

but that stinger
is still lodged
in the fat heart of my ear

as other emotions
carry through
rest in my head
lift the constraints

then reinflate to the dizzy
politics of codependent reality


. . . . .

how slyly move

the ghosts of intimacy

cool romantic entrances
blurred by
cat-like exits


. . . . .

in the zoom of power
all shifting deceptions
coercive dependencies
find their way to the forefront

then we rupture


. . . . .

these could be the
   longest nights ...
of do's
and patient arrival

citizen nowhere

climbing the ladder
beyonds scented
walls

. . . . .

what love bright shines
within the eyes
of faded fatherhood

magical maybes
    divide
the night sky

into flashbulbs
tiny and memorable


. . . . .

**ongoing love affair**

brilliant, dear

moving the way you do
through

life and me

. . . . .

# Mel Arrighi
An Ordinary Man
Daddy Pig
The Death Collection
Manhattan Gothic

# Erskine Caldwell
Estherville
Men & Women

# Christopher Morley
John Mistletoe
The Parnassus Wagon & The Haunted Bookshop
*(combined edition)*
Powder of Sympathy
Rudolph & Amina
Swiss Family Manhattan
Thunder On The Left
Where the Blue Begins

# Dorothy Salisbury Davis
A Gentle Murderer
A Gentleman Called
The Pale Betrayer

# Elizabeth Spencer
Fire in The Morning
The Night Travelers
This Crooked Way

Check out the New Titles at
www.vivisphere.com

*Henry James Forman*
The Man Who Lived in a Shoe

*Katherine Anne Dieter*
Mattie & Frank

*Dirck Van Sickle*
Montana Gothic
My Pal Rinker

*Liz Lesiak*
Mother's Blood

*James Oliver Curwood*
Nomads of the North

*George O'Har*
Psychic Fair

*Mart Baldwin*
A Busy Day In Loafer's Glory
Drifting The River
Kill The Benefactor
Over The Edge

*Frederick Manfred*
The Brother
The Giant
The Primitive
Wanderlust

*Richard Harteis*
Sapphire Dawn
Marathon

*Kevin Robinson*
A Matter of Perspective
Mall Rats
Split Seconds

*Senior Editor*
*John Paul Sinclair Lewis*

**George Catlin**
North American Indians
Vol. 1 & Vol. II

**David W. Barlett**
Joan of Arc

**William J. Bryan**
The First Battle

**Jeremiah and J.D. Chaplin**
Life of Charles Sumner

**Col. S.M. Bowman and Lt. Col. R. B. Irwin**
Sherman and His Campaigns

**Henry M. Stanley**
How I Found Livingstone

**Anonymous Wife of a Mormon Elder**
Female Life Among The Mormons

# Carrot Sky

**Senior Editor**
*Regina Wheeler*


*Robert Michael Ballantyne*
Ungava, A Tale of the Esquimaux


*James Greenwood*
Wild Sports of the World


*William J. Long*
Beasts of the Field


*Books by J. H. Fabre*
Bramble Bees and Others
Insect Life, Souvenirs of a Naturalist
Life of the Grasshopper
Social Life in the Insect World
The Glow Worm and Other Beetles
The Hunting Wasps
The Life of the Caterpillar
The Life of the Fly
The Life of the Spider
The Mason Bees
The Sacred Beetles and Others
The Story Book of Birds and Beasts
The Wonder Book of Plant Life
This Earth of Ours:
*Talks About Mountains & Rivers, Volcanoes, etc.*

### Richard Harteis
Provence

### Jim Hubert
Bone Trophies

### Terry Quinn
Mad About New York Town

### Kristopher Scuccimarra
*The Loon Box*

### Kimberly Snow
Snow - Fire and Mirth

### Lorna Tychostup
A Mirror of Flesh

### Peter Cooper
The Valley of My Eastern Heart
The Valley of My Western Heart

### Scott Cooper
Waiting to Connect

### Perry Curtis Bales
No Man Canyon
The Last Man to Kill

# Mystic Oracle

**Senior Editor**
*James Tucker*

*Jeanne Marie Antoinette*
Circle of Tears

*Daniel Logan*
Your Eastern Star

*Kelly A. Phillips*
Diary of an Anorectic

*Rev. Sunny Anne Cunningham*
The Boo Book

# UNIFONT

*Algis Budrys*
Death Machine
Falling Torch
Some Will Not Die
Who

*Catherine Mintz*
First Light
*Perry Curtis Bales*

**Max Hardy**
Standard Bridge Bidding
for the 21st Century

**Edwin B. Kantar**
A Treasury of Bridge Tips
Take Your Tricks

**David J. Weiss**
Defense At Trick One

PEABODY

**Patricia Seaton Lawford with Ted Schwarz**
The Peter Lawford Story

**Ted Schwarz**
The Hillside Strangler
Walking with the Damned

**Ted Schwarz with Ted Rybak**
Trsut No One